# THE CONNECTED FAMILY

# THE CONNECTED FAMILY

## *Strengthening Bonds in the Digital Age*

### AVERY NIGHTINGALE

Creative Quill Press

# CONTENTS

# CHAPTER 1

# Introduction

We are entering the peak years of the 21st century amidst an ongoing digital revolution that has profound implications for our social, economic, and political lives. Not surprisingly, many parents worry about what that means for their children's well-being. Recent years have seen a wave of books with comparable titles, such as "The Dumbest Generation," "Generation Me," "The Net Delusion," "The Narcissism Epidemic," and "The Shallows," that reflect a worrisome view of the digital age from the perspectives of the authors. Yet the more common worry among parents is not over whether the internet is making their children more shallow, self-centered, and gullible, but rather what they see as the root cause – the lack of meaningful family connectedness. Eighty-four percent of American adults believe that families are less close than in the past, and technology is often blamed for contributing to this decline. Indeed, survey data suggest that people turn on the television much more readily than they reach for a book whenever they find themselves with some spare time.

But though the cacophony of voices may suggest that it is now a known fact, that in actuality is uncertain. The first study that attempted to measure how digital technology affects family relationships found that teenagers who were heavy users of the internet had more trust in their mothers. Another study found that family connectedness was higher among parents and adult children who used Instagram, Snapchat, and similar photo-based media. Snapchat "may combine the visual selfie tradition with a new form of messaging that fosters social support between close friends," concluded researchers who have since become affiliated with Facebook, raising questions about possible conflicts of interest. Yet another study discovered that adolescent boys who spent more time playing video games with family members were less likely to have conduct problems. A recent report is based on data obtained from asking the same group of primarily low-income families about their internet use at an initial time point, six years later, and then 12 years after the first interview. Together, the evidence points in various directions and certainly does not support the narrative of digital technology being the bane of family relationships. Rather than taking for granted the notion that passive media consumption is a threat to family connectedness, we should be open to the possibility that active forms of technology engagement can actually enhance family relationships.

# CHAPTER 2

# Benefits of Technology in Family Life

We do, however, need to take account of the fact that it's a digital world and that doesn't seem likely to change. Children are already an important target market for many technology companies. According to UNICEF, over 175,000 children go online for the first time every day — a quarter of the world's population of young people children are online. This means that those of us who believe digital devices should—where practical—be left at the door are going to find that, for many families, when it comes to parenting this genie is already out of the bottle. At least in 'western' societies, the genie was released not, as in the tale, by rubbing a lamp, but by the arrival of the smartphone. Tech allows children to FaceTime with grandparents, find out why the sky is blue, enjoy interactive stories in multiple languages, listen to their favorite music, make films about their family, and play bridge with multiple family members.

It's not hard to see why parents might continue to seek ways of minimizing digital tech in their families. Excessive use of technology can, of course, lead to difficulties. Research shows that excessive screen time and inappropriate content can lead to mental health problems, obesity, and poor sleep in teenagers. Yet the American Academy of Pediatrics (AAP) research shows that when there are rules in place for technology use, these negative effects are negated. Other key research demonstrates that when there is a quality experience for children, digital and inter-active technologies can improve their social skills, motivation to learn, health, relationships, and happiness. Furthermore, children who are able to connect online with family and friends live a happier, healthier life. So to teach children to use the digital world responsibly means they are more likely to make healthy decisions and grow to lead a balanced lifestyle.

# CHAPTER 3

# Challenges of Technology in Family Life

The second challenge is the lack of conversation among family members when these screens light up. There was a time when families sat around the dinner table and discussed their day, strategized about tricky work situations or engaged in an impassioned debate about the qualities of their favorite sports team. Current adults tell stories of a time when they were in the midst of a sparkling story in the car with siblings or with Mom and Dad sitting on the couch at home only to look up and notice that everyone was looking into their smartphone, immersed in Facebook, Twitter, email or SMS. Most parents (both working and non-working) with children under the age of 18 feel that they don't spend enough time with their kids, according to a 2010 Pew Research Center survey. Technology that keeps kids entertained, work pressure that separates parents from children and after-school activities that engage children from parents have resulted in a 20% decline in the amount of time children spent with their parents between 1997 and 2010.

There are two major challenges facing families today that can make technology seem more like an adversary than an ally. The first is the distraction effect that digital gadgetry can have on children (and adults) who become captivated by what's on their devices' screens. Hand a crying 2-year-old a smartphone and, with any luck, the tears stop and silence ensues. But there are more dire consequences than a quiet toddler who's gotten their hands on a pacifying piece of technology. One recent study in the Journal of Pediatrics found that children aged 2 to 5 in the U.S. and Canada are using mobile media more than ever before. Another study from Pew Research Center found that 78% of teens (aged 12 to 17) own a cell phone and nearly half of them own smartphones.

# CHAPTER 4

# Establishing Healthy Digital Habits

The consistent message we send – and enforce with our children. Our daily structure is not driven by our devices and we are more present, engaged, and available. No one – adults or kids – feel perpetually connected to the office or peer pressure from social media. As a result, we have more respect and empathy for one another, navigate family conflict better, demonstrate humanness to one another, and are more in tune with one another. None of us feels the need to unplug from one another. We carry our connected family with us wherever we go. This connectedness is fueled by a bond that begins with a strong family foundation and extends to the outside world through our use of digital media. It may look like we are an attractive, happy family looking at four glowing screens. But really, our screen time is taking us back to one another and strengthening our family bonds.

The first step in addressing the effect the digital world has on the family is to evaluate your digital family habits and weaknesses. When we recognize our habits that may be affecting the connectedness of our families, we can quickly assess their purpose and look at the alternatives to pursue. By establishing some healthy habits with my family, I made sure that tech was being utilized, shared, and enjoyed, but not at the expense of meaningful face-to-face interactions. Once we established our digital habits, I realized key benefits for our family life:

# CHAPTER 5

# Communication and Connection in the Digital Age

Every new medium and platform creates new communication opportunities and challenges. Just weeks ago, Meghan Winchelle merged her love of fashion and passion for renal disease awareness to create and email a helpful flyer about career tips and match-day outfits to soon-to-be graduating medical students. Based on her daughter's enthusiasm, her mom, Jennica, decided to send the same information to her son. However, this time she used texting. Jennica did not realize that attaching all the images on her phone would make them difficult or impossible to download at the other end. Jennica tried multiple times but failed, as her daughter became increasingly upset and anxious because she believed that she was disappointing her mom. To repair a frustrating and upsetting situation, 15-year-old Alexander added value by successfully downloading and sending all images, along with a recording of himself describing three outfits. In today's connected families, communication can easily succeed or backfire due to multiple opportunities or misunderstandings with complex media and devices.

As we developed our approach to a digital lifestyle that allows for both screens and smiles, we saw an opportunity to learn more not only from our mistakes but also from the mistakes of others. Instead of trying to pave a new path to connectedness, we acknowledged the wisdom in 50-plus years of research on face-to-face connectedness. In this final section of the book, we provide more than 15 additional concrete strategies to help your family use digital tools to strengthen not just technological but also human bonds in the digital age. The tips are divided among five major categories: communication, communities, self-awareness, new media literacy, and new traditions.

# CHAPTER 6

# Balancing Screen Time and Quality Time

The 2017 Common Sense Report on Media Use by Tweens and Teens includes disturbing trends that confirm our concerns. Electronic multitasking associated with bedroom media has become common. Across platforms and devices, youth are interacting with screens for an average of 9 hours a day, excluding time on devices during classroom instruction. Common Sense's respondents indicated long-term concern about screen time patterns. For example, 38% of 13-year-olds are using social media by age 13, and 42% of teens report that they feel anxious when they don't have access to their cellphones. Concern about un-tethered access to media has resulted in research studies, recommending media contracts and requiring cell phones to be checked into a common charging station each night. These interventions encourage parents to take an authoritative, compliance-oriented stance toward teens and pre-teens as they learn self-regulated media. Establishing values that guide behavior, rather than simplistic rules, may be a better approach as we support children with developmentally appropriate media use.

Many parents are concerned about the amount of time their children and teenagers spend on digital devices. The ubiquity of internet sources of child-targeted marketing and cyberbullying gives parents new reason to worry about unsupervised media. Although we see expanded learning and engagement in social media, excess screen time is associated with physical activity deficits, inattention, and family systems problems such as scarcity of connection. The new emphasis on observing screens may seemingly relegate parent-child connections to moments when a parent takes away the screen or the screen overrides the parent's spoken message.

# CHAPTER 7

# Nurturing Emotional Well-being in a Digital World

Pediatricians can encourage parents and policymakers to design an environment that helps children grow up creating healthy relationships with media. The frustration and attempts to control the use of media in children with ADHD who have more problematic media use. Caregivers are admonished to co-use media with children to mitigate the high phonological memory load of viewing and to provide optimal learning opportunities. Parents ponder, "How are my child's developing relationships with their world changed because of media?" "Am I able to model media use that supports my child's growth and development?" "How are media, even when used for education and entertainment, potentially hurting my child?" To give parents guidance on this challenge, the AAP just released "Media and Young Minds," complementing the 2011 policy statement "Media Use by Children Younger Than Two Years" and taking fresh stock of media's impact on the health, well-being, and development of children ages zero (at birth) to eight years.

Balancing media use with other healthy behaviors has always been a challenge for parents. The new report offers recommendations for families and for pediatricians and suggests that designing a Family

Media Use Plan that considers health, education, and entertainment needs is customized to the child and family and is revisited regularly. Media are not just an inert "thing" that impacts children in a one-way direction. Media are transactional. Child development is shaped by the ongoing, reciprocal interactions that children have with their environment, of which media is a part. The cognitive development of infants and toddlers is fostered by the use of interactive 'video chat' media (i.e., with relatives or family friends). Preschoolers learn emergent literacy, especially significant for children in poverty, via joint parent-child engagement with electronic books and storybook apps.

# CHAPTER 8

# Promoting Digital Literacy and Online Safety

At the same time, research has shown that the use of the internet by children under the age of 12 is increasing. In a European survey of 25,000 parents, three-quarters of the 6- to 11-year-olds who used the internet said they were not always accompanied by an adult. On their digital devices, according to survey data from the European Commission, 71% of 9 to 16-year-olds use a camera and the internet. Children who follow their parents, who use digital technology in a family setting, are the children who have the first opportunity to learn digital competences. Recent studies show that although young children have basic digital skills, in fact, they can also evaluate digital content and express their opinions. Digital literacy skills are not easy to acquire and are rarely experienced at school. Even for those who have access to formal programs, it is unlikely that they will also receive informal support.

Educational psychologists recognize that children learn by observing the behavior and attitudes of their parents. Therefore, it is the responsibility of parents and guardians to help children comprehend and harness digital technology. Understanding how to use digital devices, develop content, and critically evaluate information and sources are basic skills. According to understanding the implications of such content, engaging with them, and knowing how to create them provides a citizen with a wide range of cognitive and collaborative skills. We also contribute to a deeper understanding of the world in which we live by developing concepts, perspectives, and judgment. The research shows that many children are, in practice, left to their own devices. Parents are just like many children, struggling with technological confusion and embarrassment.

# CHAPTER 9

# Building Trust and Openness in the Digital Era

In fact, engaging in conversations about digital media or making digital media together can be a way to close the power distance between kids and adults, recalling that parents are an important source of information and advice when it comes to media-related topics. A study on the possible ways in which not just what teens learn when they watch TV depends a great deal on discussing TV with their parents. For example, there is a higher probability that parents' willingness to hold discussions about digital media can depend on the level of involvement children display in these activities, as well as the type of devices they tend to use. Linear configurations of dispositions to media use play a similar role. Efforts may focus on narrowing these gaps. For example, findings from our multi-platform log suggest that parental co-use of digital devices and interest in trying new technologies can help promote a diverse and equitable digital era preparation among children.

Becoming digitally connected with your kids may seem at odds with the fear of them spending too much time on screens. Your intention may be to teach children about balance in the digital age and build up their resilience and self-esteem, rather than risk potentially opening up new battles by getting more involved in their digital lives. reported that the more these conversations focused on negative possibilities—cyber-bullying, sexual predators—the less likely the teens were to comfortably have them.

# CHAPTER 10

# Embracing Technology for Educational Purposes

It is essential to recognize the role of parents in the development of emerging consumer technologies. As found, "media use by kids implies a hidden role as well" (p.1807). Parents are perfect educators, advisors, mentors, and role models. They are deeply involved in children's digital lives and have a major impact on the application of media and technology for children's education. Parents should grasp how to harness the capabilities of digital media to their benefit and mitigate shortcomings. Scientific research suggests that appropriate media use, including technology designed for education and for students and families to use together, could be relevant to children's cognitive and literacy growth. strongly believes that the role of parents in enhancing healthy media experiences with children cannot be overlooked.

Kids today are naturally wired for technology. More than ever, parents are starting to adapt to this new age of digital advancement and become increasingly connected to the digital world. A recent study reported that American teenagers between the ages of 13 and 18, on average, spend their time using more than nine hours of media a day. With the reported upsurge in educational technology, it is important that parents are prepared to guide their children to develop the aware, mindful, and tech-savvy citizenry of the 21st century. Given this digital era, many parents wonder how much technology is suitable for their kids, how much time children should engage with the different tools available, and what suitable educational activities are suggested for increasing children's technological skills.

# CHAPTER 11

# Strengthening Family Bonds through Shared Digital Experiences

The authors ask the critical research question "Considering the impact of digital technologies on our daily lives, how do the ways we use them separately or together bring family members closer or pull them apart?" The authors build on previous research the study of technology use through the lens of social practices, which examines how people in social groups, such as the family, create feelings and meanings of relationship closeness through their practices of everyday family life. Dervin coined this connective action. Within the context of family, connective action allows family members to understand their interdependence and interconnections nominal. By using theories of connective action, partial connective action, and disruptions of connective action when mooring the concept of technology use to that of connecting or disconnecting, the authors extend Dervin's work of connective action to digital technologies used by family members.

The vast literature on digital technologies and screen time illustrates that the topic carries a lot of weight in today's society. We know that screen time exceeds six hours each day, effectively making multimedia devices primary socializers and communicators. Our familiarity with new technologies, their affordances, and the power and problems they manifest are, therefore, daily and growing at an exponential rate. At the fundamental level of the nuclear family, digital screens are often cited as powerful tools that simultaneously tear families apart through their isolating and individualizing characteristics, yet keep families together as a node of family life, work, and leisure. Although many families report that they use technologies to strengthen familial bonds, we also wonder how, and how well, this is done. Is the volume of contact and communication, while facilitating certain aspects of family life, taking away from family members' "sense of the other"? In this chapter, we assessed whether technology use (over and above its mere existence or volume) enhances family connectedness.

# CHAPTER 12

# Cultivating Mindfulness and Presence in the Digital Age

In the theoretical literature, connectedness and presence are important areas for literature. Theories explain the best human ways to connect with each other and to be present while being together. To address technology's potential negative impacts in families, and to cope with the paradox and cultivate the healthy and real bonding opportunities, we need strategies and techniques that foster proper connectedness and presence within the family network. To accomplish this, the theoretical literature guides us on how to develop the capacity of being mindful and present in a higher quality level, and on how to be aware of the connectedness principles maintaining the best level of human ways of connecting and relating to each other. This article explores the possibilities of two complementary approaches: presence and mindfulness as defined by their founders and as discussed in new ways in the context of digital technology by recent scholars. Drawing from both sets of principles, we then forward a set of recommendations, building on practices that are suitable for various family members: parents, children, and children at various ages, as ever-growing users, to be more mindful and present in the digital age. Such practices aim to enable better family-related digital technology use for preserving the quality of life and connection within the family network.

Cell phones, the internet, and other communication technologies connect family members in new ways, increasing the opportunities and places for developing lifelong bonds. However, the same technologies can also isolate individuals and family members from one another. Mobile and digital tools often distract family members, diverting their attention away from each other and disrupting real-world connections. Parents sometimes miss out on their children's activities and cues, which are essential for connection and understanding. But, neither is the connection fully established when we are together. In a family setting that is supposed to maximize the connection time, technology is becoming a significant distraction. Distractiveness is not the only issue associated with technology use; also problematic is the way that mobile or digital tools impact the family's quality time. Parents sometimes miss the important moments, activities, or cues of their children, causing them to suffer from miscommunication and misinterpretation. All these missing points and gaps prevent the possibility of understanding, connection, interaction, and bonding within the family network. Because of this, as part of the connectivity paradox, technology hinders the actual bonding opportunities while it provides various ways to connect.

# CHAPTER 13

# Fostering Creativity and Imagination in a Digital World

To enrich a child's imagination, take away their digital devices, then either have them create a character in physical world play (life, too; if their instinct is to make a 'mini-me,' resist advising them - young children often see colors in skin, hair, and attire and bring in mind a person they associate with those elements), have a parent read a child a book or talk to the child about a story they have read, or go to a museum or zoo and with the aid of a museum or zoo staff person, discuss how different iconic animals might appear or behave given the problems and environments that make them unique. When a question arises, suggest they think about it for themselves, if appropriate.

Parents who are in the tech field are typically those who can do family digital upbringing well and cover all the educational bases. This allows them not to worry about the Bruner camps and Orbis and engage those camps' excellent materials as time and finances allow. Besides immersive and engaging games (Crayola Scoot, Dora & Diego Let's Explore for preschoolers, SimCity, Civilization for older preschoolers and up), there are countless apps and simple real-world activities that can recapture a child's imagination and help solve a pressing household problem. What digital and digital-like activities are not currently solving is the problems that are going astray; civics and American society are in a free-fall; social skills need cultivation as group empathy and decades of social education are going downhill fast; and the great questions are...

In our connected culture, deploying technology to effectively feed curiosity and sharpen critical thinking is essential. Preschool children, for example, are now spending nearly twice as much time watching TV or playing video games as they are reading with a family member. While they are seeing a leap in peripheral vision, as well as more engagement in the things they do and hear (such as jumping when they see Nintendo's Super Mario leaping, or seeing the width of a crevice widen as they approach it), the creative brain development that is more engaged while children read a story is at rest - even when one of the new interactive children's books is read to a child from an e-book reader. With a paper book, the child is listening to the adult, discovering the words on the page, the illustrations, and using their imagination to see what the characters look like, the movement in between the frames that illustrate an action, and the excitement in the story's pacing. Digital books give the child all those things, removing the play between the adult's voice and the specific lessons within the structures of the storytelling, as well as promoting more distraction as they assess the other active options in a digital universe. Creative play through free-form block, finger painting, and imaginative games are also at risk while children play with emotive robots, or games and toys designed around franchises where conflict is the educational platform.

# CHAPTER 14

# Encouraging Physical Activity and Outdoor Play

So how can parents encourage their young ones to engage in more physical activity and outdoor play? Here are a few strategies: Prohibit digital activity while working in the family yard. Clearing the leaves off the sidewalk should not be delegated to the young ones alone, as parents sit in the house and watch TV. Parents can involve their children in a variety of family activities that take place outside. The best way to encourage positive behavior in children is through example. Thus parents, who are active outdoors, practice organic farming with compost, take part in conservation projects, ride their bikes, hike, camp, fish and play toss games, can have an impact on children. While for many families, it may not be feasible, sometimes entirely removing the source of temptation (computer, TV, game console) can not only be beneficial to the child/family relationships, but can also be a gateway to initiating more outdoor play when options are limited. With more time allowed for outdoor play, kids are able to develop an appreciation for nature as well as emotional and social skills.

Over the last 10 years, more children have been spending time immersed in digital activities. According to a report by the Kaiser Family Foundation, between the years 1999 and 2009, average time spent on digital activities by 8- to 18-year-olds increased from 3 hours and 1 minute to 6 hours and 21 minutes a day. A University of Michigan report of 3,500 4th through 6th graders in 2009 revealed that a vast majority of these students were spending ten or more hours weekly engaged in sedentary activities - watching TV and playing video, computer and hand-held games. These findings taken alongside similar reports paint a troublesome picture. Howard Taras, professor of pediatrics at the University of California at San Diego School of Medicine sums it up well as he suggests that there might be "detrimental long-term consequences due to screens," including loss of sleep and opportunities to exercise in the outdoors.

# CHAPTER 15

# Managing Digital Distractions and Overstimulation

Debby Miller, an associate of Jackson on the Pioneer Institute, jumbles her two roles by coping with a habit called "captive, trapped to a specific place". Accumulating a host of statistics, both by her own survey and from the reports of Pew Research Centre, an apparent verdict concurs that very many Americans feel spiky in response to electronic gadgets, their medium of distractions, magnified overstimulation, and divides which encroach yet privacy. "Just checking in once in a while" made up 28 people of the polled adults, a third of this figured admitted to being chronic desktop captives, another quarter were Blackberry "captives" by yet realization, and a fifth composed Smartphone "captives". Even being called in companionable circles did not alleviate their awkwardness. Miller did not let the Wireless_User circle off either; they suffered a worse fate, pipping all others. "84% of them confined to this vagabond ambience, unfettered by cable circuits, voiced their anxieties over its intrusiveness in homespun environments."

Maggie Jackson, herself a working mother, knows that the prolific power of electronic media could threaten to wreck family dynamics, overtaking personal priorities, and eroding togetherness. However,

Maggie does not bulldoze her pessimism on readers. Instead, she tackles the pitfalls of online living with passion and thorough analysis before offering strategy and prospects. Jackson tells us a disconcerting story of a mother, Christie Kittelsen, who habitually checks work messages while at home, neglecting her children's talking and the haunting call of maternal worries whenever she heard them stop their giggles outside her door. As young as 10-year-old Alex already refused to accompany her when she went out just because "she might hear the Blackberry beep".

# CHAPTER 16

# Empowering Parents as Digital Role Models

The parental role in youth digital life has a unique flavor and up-shot. For one, parents act as gatekeepers to technology. A 2016 study involving 141 participants aged 16–25 found that the parental wages regarding social media networking, content creation, and being part of e-forums significantly impacted the children's behavior. Further, a second study involving 81 individuals in the same age range discovered that parents' self-disclosure policies in social media significantly established the children's practice of creating a positive digital footprint. Such positions taken by parents when deciding what can be done with technology, whose ideas take precedence, and whom we connect with and how, give parents the responsibility of laying down the framework for appropriate digital conduct, and the opportunity to speculate, understand, and adopt what youthful technology exploration might mean and require.

The other part deals with digital mentoring, a practice that promotes adult-imbued skills and ethical online behavior. This idea involves a mentor or coach who takes time to share fun activities that improve a positive digital footprint, model teachable moments for others, and foster creativity in children by demonstrating ways to communicate with stoops of inspiration, criticism, and creativity in online forums.

Given the importance of positive digital engagement in the lives of children and youth, the question becomes, how can adults adopt constructive, fun, and effective tech habits around children? Part of the solution lies in acknowledging that good parenting hasn't changed, yet the challenges and possibilities have, and that if kids are going to think critically about what they consume—and contribute to—the digital environment, we need to model for them how to engage with these tools in thoughtful ways. And if we don't understand a tech activity or perspective a child is interested in, we must take a moment to learn about it.

# CHAPTER 17

# Overcoming Generational Gaps in Technology Use

Conversely, older adults often wish to use technology to support their social relationships, but must rely on others to teach them how. One tension between older and younger generations is how exactly to do that. Lund's research participants frequently tell her that their adult children will only lay out their digital tools for them, while the person who wishes to learn needs someone to stand by and assist as they gain the comfort and abilities to navigate the internet. Levine points out that we're only dabbling in the deeper work of developing tools to close the intergenerational technology learning gap. If an older person bought a Mac desktop in 1984 and found the interface straightforward, he would likely purchase a Mac again. Unfortunately, each tool iteration since—"the first Windows interface, a Palm Pilot, the first iTunes"—makes it difficult for this person to learn newer computers, tablet devices, or smartphones.

Common knowledge suggests that older Americans are the ones who struggle with technology use. Although some older people do grapple with tech, age does not, in fact, dictate comfort with it. In 2016, a survey noted that 84 percent of Americans ages 60-69 have a smartphone (in contrast, about 92 percent of the general population have smartphones), and the senior market will be the most rapidly growing tech-consumer group. Still, the stereotype of older people's ignorance persists, and can be a wedge driven between generations. Berkeley Lund, a professor of Communication at North Dakota State University, says in many young people's studies of technology use, the "value system isn't about what older people do already; it's about what young people can do with it."

# CHAPTER 18

# Promoting Healthy Sleep Habits in the Digital Era

At this time, the electronic media-sleep relation mostly remains shrouded in questions. Different parts of the youth population likely vary in how digital media use affects sleep, as adolescents in different developmental periods, who exhibit diverse behavioral traits, and who have varying amounts of emotional and learning skills, will use media differently. Similarly, media experiences could affect sleep differently (e.g., worrisome dreams and nighttime awakenings could be underscored by horror movies and gaming involving virtual violence). Although intensive electronic media use that crowds out sleep and reduces youths' alertness occurs during the nighttime, digital media use during the day also can have negative ramifications for the sleep patterns of families. With appropriate parental oversight, the cavalier use of media by adolescents could provide fertile soil for electronic media to take root in the bedrooms of those who first use media. Household media use preaches as strongly as family media use. Following the limitation of digital media use to specific areas of the home, households could emphasize family quarters, leading children and older others alike to better detangle themselves from the digital devices and offering them the chance to experience the blessings of the increased levels of family togetherness that blossom under these media consumption habits. As such, media use could be particularly intertwined with adolescent sleep when the trajectories of digital media use and the places of dwindling-needed—yet difficult to arrange—family togetherness spike in synchronicity in families. Yet regardless of their technologic intimate state, youth will continue to look to adults for guidance, especially when they are in the twilight of confusion and feel warm and safe in the cozy confines of family.

The importance of sleep cannot be overstated, and yet much of the world appears to be in the midst of a silent epidemic of sleep loss. Driving trends of sleep loss include the internet, social media, video gaming, and mobile devices, all of which can be particularly enticing to youths. Thus far, youth and parents may surmise that digital media use is related to only minor sleep disturbances, such as a few lost minutes of rest each night. Yet in the aggregate, these minutes become hours, especially in view of the fact that adolescents already are at risk of shortened sleep durations. Moreover, data from a diverse and multiethnic sample of American children in middle childhood hint that future generations could be at risk for experiencing substantial amounts of lost sleep, as media use has rapidly become a staple behavior during the child development process. The complex allure of digital technology will present a persistent challenge as youths and families struggle to maintain good-quality rest in an era filled with electronic devices.

# CHAPTER 19

# Harnessing Technology for Family Organization and Productivity

Parents would be wise to also integrate an online family planner like the Cozi app in their household. This is a particularly comprehensive resource and a personal favorite. You can input meal plans, activities, recipes, and shopping lists all in one place. Ideally, kids can assist in meal planning too, identifying what they like and dislike, perhaps even acting as sous chefs!

Additionally, parents alleviating the numerous responsibilities they have on their plate should certainly employ Google Keep to-do lists and grocery lists. Both allow for individual to-do's to be divided amongst members using the same Google account. As the children complete items on the list, they can check them off and all individuals on the account will be alerted as to what has been completed.

Google Calendar is an accessible app, both across iOS and Android devices, that allows your family to easily schedule and see all of your events in one place. The left pane of the app allows you to toggle family members on and off to view the events that are relevant to each individual. This is a particularly beneficial tool with older children, who can involve themselves in the planning process, and it is excellent for keeping nannies or babysitters informed of the family's whereabouts.

A connected family is an organized family. The demands of everyday life often lead to disorder and unrest, especially when you throw children into the mix. All parents can relate to the feeling of chaos that ensues with the numerous activities and work schedules, doctors' appointments, play dates, and household chores to tackle. As such, families should consider employing the multiple features of technology, such as Google's suite of tools, for smooth and efficient organization.

# CHAPTER 20

# Addressing Cyberbullying and Online Harassment

Children who are cyberbullied may not want to talk about it with their parents out of embarrassment. It's crucial to pick a time when everyone is calm to talk and to express concern rather than anger or judgment. Children may also feel guilty, embarrassed, or ashamed about being cyberbullied and resist reporting their experience because they may feel they somehow are deserving of what happened. They also might be concerned that by reporting the harassment, they will be prohibited from using their electronic devices altogether. The U.S. Department of Justice suggests that parents get as much information from their child without forcing a detailed conversation. This way, they can pursue an investigation responsibly and legally. While taking the child's device and removing it from the Internet might seem like a quick fix, parents should allow their child to keep the device to continue documenting the harassing behavior.

Cyberbullying is when someone repeatedly harasses, mistreats, or makes fun of another person online or while using cell phones or other electronic devices. Cyberbullies have used websites such as Facebook, Twitter, or other social networking sites, as well as emails, instant messaging, and cell phone texting to unleash their attacks. It's important to remember that when a child commits cyberbullying, their parents may be held legally responsible if the child being bullied is under age 18. Parents can face civil or criminal penalties (or both) if the child's online conduct results in injury, death, or significantly disrupts a child's education, and the parents had the ability to prevent the child's conduct, had made reasonable attempts to prevent the conduct, and had taken zero action to prevent further abusive conduct. If the child is between ages 18 and 24, the parents may still be held civilly liable.

# CHAPTER 21

# Supporting Positive Online Relationships and Friendships

The transition from motivational to meaningful relies on being thoughtful in the ways that we interact. It is not enough to simply spend time together. That time has to be well spent. Many researchers, including University of Virginia psychologist Joseph Allen and associates, have found that there is a relationship between the depth of conversation and the support that teens gain during the conversation. Positive online interactions like hobbies, video games, and even casual conversation can be ways that kids develop these positive online relationships. Ask what your child is doing and offer guidance and information to them as they interact and play. Participate in the interactions when/if invited to learn more about who they are as a connected person.

The benefits of cultivating friendships online are significant. Online friendships can support children's social development and help young people develop early skills that are instrumental to future success. Though less common, these virtual connections can also offer some special benefits. They enable digital kids to share their interests and passions with people who they might not have access to in the physical world. Through their connections with friends who share common causes or interests, kids can collaborate in ways that facilitate new learning, which can be especially powerful given the current pace of change in the lives of digital youth. When asked to consider the ways friendships with adults influence youth positively, Heidi G. and David C., a research and evaluation director and a district coordinator, reasoned that some of these same benefits result when youth have nurturing, caring relationships with people who are not their parents. It is only reasonable to imagine that the same would be true if their relationship is a primarily digital one.

# CHAPTER 22

# Respecting Privacy and Digital Boundaries

In the well-known digital documentary, most people who agreed to allow the movie to access their browser history had a problem with the site accessing or utilizing the information that was available to them. In the digital age, most people in your house probably freely access or use your digital footprint. Can you do things to protect it? Sure. But the easiest way to protect you and your kids from nefarious activities is keeping an eye on the traffic in and out of your house. If you inform your kids of the reasons behind your prying eyes and never make them feel like you are cracking down on them and only trying to protect them, the boundaries in the house will be clearer.

As kids grow up, they typically become more private and want to develop their own social circles. It wouldn't be good if parents stalked them. But the key is respect, not privacy. Any adult in a child's life is allowed to have information to keep them safe. Most parents wouldn't be upset if a teacher or coach informed them of an incident at school or the rink. That conversation likely happened because their child was changing or doing something that suggested something wrong was going on. When those things start happening in the digital world, the same rules should apply. There should be no selected surprises. But this is just part one of respecting a child's digital privacy. The key is respecting their boundaries and having honest discussions when there are problems.

# CHAPTER 23

# Dealing with Digital Addiction and Dependency

We're making a choice to support the rising rates of childhood obesity to historic levels instead of setting clear boundaries. We're making a choice to undermine our children's potential in emotional intelligence, using their inner thoughts and feelings to help them, instead of leaving it underdeveloped and lacking verbal communication. We know it is possible to moderate our children's media consumption, as proven by the scores of young people who have never used smartphones and video games. Children who interact with parents frequently and have lots of activities in real life are not at risk for digital dependency or addiction. Instead, they thrive. You can take these two real-life examples as lessons. The risks are clear when we refuse to take action together as a family to moderate screen time, so the family can grow strong with digital natives.

Parents often ask me if their children can really get addicted to the internet. My response is that while I'm not a psychiatrist or a certified addictions counselor, I see what I call digital dependency, and I believe that dependence resembles a child's defiance. The quality of time online and with screens is the measure of how attached and dependent children become on looking at flat screens. Whether children are viewing television screens, movie screens, laptops, or iPads, digital media has become our default setting for entertainment, without realizing and without knowing we're making a choice.

# CHAPTER 24

# Encouraging Critical Thinking and Media Literacy

The real promise of the connected family, as books and "pot-boiler" articles about the digital age alike accurately boast, is the dizzying cornucopia of apps that can help raise your kids. Bored as you drive to soccer practice? In the old days, adults urged that you look out the window at the world, but today that's probably only getting a kid's hopes up for little gain. Far better to hand them a digital device. There they will be likely to find not mere empty relaxation, the usual charge against television watching, but the infinite and educational pleasure of the digital world as they single-mindedly play (virtuous and enriching) concentration-building games or watch (virtuous and enriching) mini-films. Want to calm or reward a kid? Audio books are just the ticket. There are dozens of apps for parents trying to make the best of life as a constantly harassed multitasker.

Encouraging critical thinking and media literacy is a priority for connected parents. Simply put, this means we want our children not just to consume media, but to think about it as well. When they watch a commercial, we want them to be alert to its possible motives, the sorts of people it targets and how, and the persuasive tricks it employs—such as catchy jingles, scratch and sniff perfume ads in magazines, or faded film stock to make old-fashioned things like ice cream makers or turn-of-the-century clothes seem more "authentic" or "wholesome." We can also substitute more complex interpretations for simple ones that may be presented in something they are watching. For example, in the movie "The Incredibles," the evil villain, we are supposed to understand, is using technology to undermine our faith in ourselves and so foster a sense of dependency. We might point out, however, that the real threat she personifies is not technology per se but a stunted moral intelligence that creates people who pamper their kids so much that they send them out into the world unprepared to fend for themselves, unaware that the freedom to fail or to excel is at the very heart of what makes us who we are.

# Exploring Virtual Reality and Augmented Reality in Family Life

As Tim said, Andy and I are finally feeling the effects of the way we've chosen to live our working life on our home life, specifically how we hope to share our work with Seb. We have no timelines here. We've met a lot of people at Microsoft who are doing great work in VR in healthcare, then come home and don't expose their kids to VR at all because they're worried about the health effects. We've also met a lot of people in the XR community in general who are proud to have their kids play with development hardware. We're somewhere in the middle. For one, we don't have headsets lying around the house in reach of a toddler who occasionally wants to pick things up. Second, we feel strongly that the content and context that Seb experiences through augmented reality - or any technology - is what will shape him, not just the technology itself.

These apps and experiences represent the cutting edge of VR and AR, but we believe there's more going on here than what's found on a screen. It's the digital context these experiences rely on that's the stuff of the future: asynchronous 3D communication, new ways of collaboration and expression, new forms of tapestry of connection through ambient in-the-background-together-ness (these are the best words I can find to describe this - it's the state of being together while talking and acknowledging each other, and isn't just being together just without intentional conversation... but there's no definitive word yet for that last one, and we need one). What discoveries will we make? What social cues will evolve in these new spaces? How will we express ourselves when some of our words and objects exist, yes, in the same space as our bodies but with degrees of separation or difference that don't exist in real life? I can't wait to find out.

# CHAPTER 26

# Navigating Social Media and Online Identity

Online identity. Developing a digital profile and reputation is important for online and offline opportunities. The required components involve privacy, their online identity, and their reputation. Encourage kids to think of reputation as what will matter to future colleges, employers, and relationships. It's important to be both real and reflective rather than impulsive when it comes to sharing content. When kids come to you asking to create social media profiles, make sure they take their time to consider what they will be sharing. Make sure they understand it is okay to censor themselves, to protect themselves. Profiles that may reveal a little too much about their personal lives are protected appropriately. Additionally, help them understand that what they put on the internet can stay with them for a long time and that it will impact their future in ways we still can't completely understand. A reckless selfie can end a teen's future career. Protect them but let them grow – let them develop their ethics but realize that helping them learn to censor themselves is a part of protecting their identity.

Media balance: Stay informed. Keep an open dialogue with your child about their social media worlds. Express an interest in what your kids see, participate in, and how they're using social media. Encourage responsible behavior. This involves treating others with compassion and conducting oneself thoughtfully. Before considering the dos and don'ts of social media guidelines, the same core positions we used with other gadgets still apply – posture, the 20-20-20 rule, and turn-taking around sharing connected things. Self-expression. Create opportunities and environments where kids feel safe to express themselves in their unique ways.

Navigating social media and online identity. Social media is an integral part of your child's life, and love it or hate it, it's not going away. Kids use social media to connect with their peers, their community, and their favorite celebrities. Young people rely on apps and websites to communicate with friends in real time, plan events, and share selfies. The benefits of social media are also real, ranging from finding support for health challenges (like meditation and grief help) to fundraising for humanitarian causes. It also gives kids a platform to share their passions about issues they care about. These are some of the benefits of social media, but challenges with information management and digital relationships remain. Ultimately, social media provides an opportunity to give our children a broader view of the world. It's an opportunity for them to begin to understand alternative perspectives on issues, events happening globally and locally, and to begin to understand who they are as people in the context of these broader things. However, challenges exist, and maintaining a balance remains something parents will need to support.

# CHAPTER 27

# Managing Online Gaming and Screen Time Limits

Timothy Wilson, Coleen Mills, and Nancy Stein state that the presence of screen-time limits can have a direct influence on a child's experience with media. In the presence of screen time limits, children have reported improved self-control, and have been found to have small but significant less-measurable impulsivity in their ability to shape their online action. Johnrate Ospina and Sarai Garcia ascribe reductions in child tantrums from family-enforced screen time limits on associated self-regulated behavior. Uhls also found that "having the rules of behavior in mind while playing can positively affect self-regulatory behavior" alluding to reduced or no extreme reactions of anger or frustration. She found that with clear delineation of gaming time and desired self-creation, gaming became an enjoyable activity allowing children to better control their lives. These influences may be particularly relevant in the health context in child 28.active gaming and potential cognitive development and increase in academic performance. As Wilson and Back note, observations show that online gaming can foster ability in the development of reasoning skills which allow children to better demonstrate persistence while utilizing data among other emotions, cognitive development, 30.socialize in moral reasoning. For example, positive relationships between a recent "spike" in online play and latent factor scores in responsible use have been observed, suggesting an intrinsic relationship between online video game play and responsibility in family communication. Other observations speak to how academic outcome can directly benefit from time spent in learning skillful persistence; family shared time including schoolwork "implicitly encourages activities such as homework, reading, and school projects," further encouraging academic purpose and a potential end to disengagement.

Both Sherry Turkle and Yalda T. Uhls note that rules can be particularly helpful for managing online gaming. Turkle states that kids (age-license for gaming or not) will benefit from limits, and she recommends putting practices in place prior to adolescents becoming heavily absorbed in the online gaming world. Uhls walked with her middle school-aged son through negotiations and time-limits and maintained involvement in his ongoing video game life. Both Turkle and Uhls emphasize that it is important to be open to negotiating any rule in the family. Uhls recommends having an actual written contract, a practice common at her former job as an entertainment industry CEO, that lays out careful, defined, time-based constraints. These "are critical in the tween and teen years, and allow children to take control of the more attractive and exciting activities and learn the self-management of time as per rules the parents set." Turkle also suggests that if this family rule were agreed upon digitally, it illustrated children's high respect for family contracts in all parts of their lives. During the early years, open family conversations about acceptable entertainment time limits can produce the best practices to represent family values, according to Turkle.

# CHAPTER 28

# Promoting Empathy and Kindness in Digital Interactions

Recent research suggests that what's most important for children's emotional and psychological development is whether digital interactions promote the different aspects of well-being and positive functioning – that is, whether we talk to and truly engage with our digital stakeholders (friends and family), asking about their thoughts and experiences, showing appreciation, providing a hand of support or comfort in tough times, all things that are also part of empathy and kindness. While this study participants were college students, and their smartphone interactions depended on less subtle, less immediate modes of communication than the ones our children mostly use, we can learn a few lessons from the outcomes. We can validate adolescents' sense of autonomy by keeping our smartphone rules at a minimum and mindful of the actual needs of well-being, the internet may be an unjust place that impairs well-being, but it is also a place where children can learn to develop and show empathy and kindness to friends, family, and the world, to find and connect with those who understand and validate their feelings of anxiety and pain, and to find infinite ways of self-expression and creativity. Our task is to work with them in assessing risks and rewards and promoting the latter.

There is no one-size-fits-all rule when deciding the right time to give a child a smartphone, not just because every child develops at their own pace, but because the answer depends in large part on the child's assessment of and willingness to address the risks and the rewards. It is helpful to remember that along with the risks and costs, digital technologies also provide our children new opportunities to build relationships with friends, family, and the rest of the world. As parents and caregivers, when we focus too much on safety or limit a child's opportunities to build relationships, we run the risk of hindering children's ability to reach out to those near or far when they feel the need.

# CHAPTER 29

# Understanding the Impact of Digital Media on Child Development

How digital media is harnessed and its impact will likely depend on the age and amount of use by the child; it can assist learning, expose the child to detrimental and even harmful content, and lead children to addiction. In their book, "The Apps for Children Advertised on Google Play: Evidence-Based Information about the Online Promotion of Apps that can be used by Children younger than Two Years Old," Krcmar, Zhou, Wilson, and Moore (2020) found that despite demonstrating the dangers associated with young children using apps on Google's Play Store that were not child-friendly, there was an increase in the number of applications and the number of downloads from the Play Store and other online sources that were associated with these dangers. Therefore, it is important for parents, educators, and scientists to monitor and control digitally-mediated learning by young children.

The effect of digital technology on child development is complex and individually variable. A balanced view of the situation embraces both the positive and the negative aspects of exposure to digital media. Digital technology's impact on children consists of two components: what they do with it and how long they engage with it. In 2010,

Common Sense Media reported that children and teens up to 8 and 18 years, respectively, spent on average 1 hour and 59 minutes daily using digital media (media multitasking was taken into account). In 2017, that same group spent 18 minutes more, or a daily total of 2 hours and 16 minutes using digital media. The increased amount of time spent by children under eight years using digital media that occurred in just over six years calls for thinking about the impact of digital technology on child development.

# CHAPTER 30

# Supporting Special Needs Children in the Digital Age

Autism is an area that has been particularly well-studied by the academic community. As the National Initiative of the National Library of Medicine declares, "No one instructional-based intervention is superior" and applications that are "working today" are available at their web pages. A number of the organizations within the NLM program relate, however, to exercise, nutrition, and health, while only a few relate to medical information specifically. According to a recent Pew Research Survey, majorities of everyone - readers of all ages, races, sexes, education, social, internet, phone, and experience; each of each and all of all at rates of twenty per cent and above - have sought health information in the last year. In contrast, the same study also finds that only 12% of Internet users have ever gone online for advice, support, or personal information in regards to autism serving as an example of a health-related activity.

Children with special needs have challenges that few others can understand the full complexity of. Imagine, however, how helpful school assignments, resource information, or materials from guest speakers could become: "What about the child that cannot write at all, types slowly and then struggles to edit, save, and email... Sounds simple, but is a backbreaking ordeal to accomplish." For the person with disabilities, technology has long been a means to offer mainstream access to activities in ways they could not have previously done. We all benefit from their use of technology; Dr. Gaddy Weathersby is one of the leading engineering-focused academics in programs to assist students with physical disabilities. In addition to ongoing individual student assistance and teaching, their actions have offered technology to make significant changes in the ways that stars have successfully managed both challenges and opportunities.

# CHAPTER 31

# Exploring Online Learning and Remote Education

At its core, learning is about making a meaningful connection between two critical areas in a child's environment: home and school. There is a well-established connection between parents and student learning, which is often referred to as the home-school connection. More meaningful parent involvement leads to increased student motivation, improved behavior, and a more positive attitude toward education overall. Researchers have found that although there are many extrinsic or internal rewards of learning, the strongest skill a student can develop is a strong connection or bond with his or her parents or caregivers. Studies show that when parents stop being involved with their kids on a level deeper than simply monitoring and rewarding, especially during middle school, kids are less likely to learn—that is, they are less likely to strengthen the "ties that bind" between home and school. Lengthy time and intensive commitment to our kids strengthen those bonds, deepening our communication channels for learning. As a result, our children are more likely to flourish in school.

There are significant benefits to online interactive learning, particularly for older children, including a high level of student engagement and learning content that is personally relevant to them. Teachers can be more effective in creating an engaging and effective learning experience when they incorporate students' passions and interests into the curriculum. When a student actively seeks out and explores specific videos and content, they are more fully engaged in the learning process. In a 2009 meta-analysis of 46 studies, educational psychologist Richard Mayer found that well-designed educational video promotes effective use of working memory by off-loading information.

# CHAPTER 32

# Conclusion

Technology will continue to propose educational and digital entertainment solutions, but unless one chooses to take a driving seat, the potential of relationships may not be utilized to its fullest. Therefore, respecting the values of providing children an experience-filled world, constructiveness despite all technology offers and purpose, and time should alter concerning attitudes, routines, and beliefs. Opportunities of togetherness must be exploited immediately, before virtual reality can destroy comprehensible real life. More connection time offers increased happiness and better relationships and gives space to focus on human-existential elements that really matter in life. A unified family will play an integral role in fighting social media virtual friendships and self-conceptualization due to the trial and errors these social media utilize.

Society is at a crossroads, where people are very digitally connected to information and disconnected from one another. The American family, in particular, finds themselves struggling to connect or have conversation. With the average child, aged 2-17, spending 7.5 hours a day on media devices and using them for both entertainment and homework, people are sacrificing relationship quality for online networks. This book provides an understanding of the negative devastating effects and the potential destructive effects of digital over-digitalization on family life and personal relationships. Not only does this book delimit the severity of the harmful outcomes one experiences when deprived of healthy, meaningful relationships, but this book also offers proposals of solutions to restore and foster connectivity between family members. By abiding by the guidance within this book, one can improve family relationships and take part in the power of "human-matters-connection" rather than forfeit deep connections for access to the endless abyss of information on the World Wide Web.

www.ingramcontent.com/pod-product-compliance
Lightning Source LLC
Chambersburg PA
CBHW051455140726
47987CB00006B/2719